Let's Talk About Having Asthma

Elizabeth Weitzman

Heinemann
LIBRARY

First published in Great Britain by Heinemann Library,
Halley Court, Jordan Hill, Oxford OX2 8EJ,
a division of Reed Educational & Professional Publishing Ltd.

OXFORD FLORENCE PRAGUE MADRID ATHENS MELBOURNE AUCKLAND
KUALA LUMPUR SINGAPORE TOKYO IBADAN NAIROBI KAMPALA JOHANNESBURG
GABORONE PORTSMOUTH NH (USA) CHICAGO MEXICO CITY SAO PAOLO

First edition © The Rosen Publishing Group, Inc. 1997
This edition © Reed Educational & Professional Publishing Ltd 1998

Manufactured in the United States of America.

02 01 00 99 98
10 9 8 7 6 5 4 3 2 1
ISBN 0431 03598 9

British Library Cataloguing in Publication Data
Weitzman, Elizabeth
Let's talk about having asthma
1. Asthma in children - Juvenile literature
I. Title II. Having asthma
618.9'2'238

Acknowledgements
The Publishers would like to thank the following for permission to reproduce photographs:
Cover photo, page 12, page 15 and page 20 © Allen & Hanburys.
All other photo illustrations by Carrie Ann Grippo.
Our thanks to Mandy Ross in the preparation of this edition.
Every effort has been made to contact copyright holders of any material reproduced in this book.
Any omissions will be rectified in subsequent printings if notice is given to the Publisher.

Contents

Words in **bold letters like these** are explained in the Glossary on pages 22 and 23.

Jacob

After he'd scored a goal in the football game, Jacob had to stop playing. All of a sudden, he couldn't breathe. Then he started coughing, which made breathing even harder. His coach came running over. 'Are you okay, Jacob?' he asked.

Jacob had been playing football for three years. Sometimes he coughed a lot when he ran too fast, but it had never been this bad before. He was scared. What was wrong with him?

It's frightening when it's hard to breathe.

What is asthma?

Like thousands of other children and grown-ups, Jacob has asthma. When he ran too hard and too fast during his football game, he had an asthma **attack**.

When someone has asthma, his or her **lungs** don't always work as well as other people's. We use our lungs to breathe. We breathe all the time without thinking about it. But if you have asthma, sometimes it can get harder for you to breathe.

Your lungs are working even when you don't realize it. ▶

Who gets asthma?

Anybody can have asthma. Often, several people in a family have it. If someone in your family has asthma, it doesn't mean you're certain to get it. But if you have asthma, there's probably someone else in your family who has it too.

People who have asthma often have **allergies** too. This means that they may get a rash or start to sneeze if they come across certain things, such as dust or pets. This is called a bad **reaction**.

People who have asthma often have allergies too.

Asthma attacks

Most of the time, you probably won't even notice that you have asthma. But from time to time you may have an asthma **attack**. It may be caused by eating a food you're **allergic** to. Or it may be caused by exercising too hard.

During an attack, you may feel as though you can't breathe. If you try to breathe harder or faster, you'll start to feel weak or dizzy. You may not be able to stop coughing, and your chest may hurt.

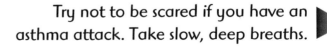
Try not to be scared if you have an asthma attack. Take slow, deep breaths.

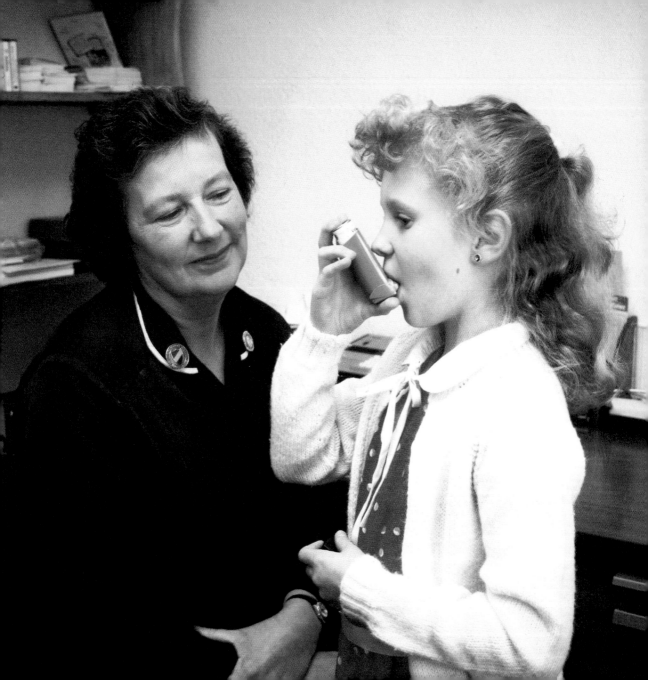

Having an asthma attack

Having an asthma **attack** can be very frightening. But the best thing you can do is to try to stay calm. It may be hard, but staying calm will help your breathing to get easier. It will also make you better able to remember to take your **medication**.

Find a grown-up to help you when you have an asthma attack. Your mum, dad, teacher or coach will stay with you until you can breathe more easily again.

A grown-up can help you with your asthma medication.

Asthma medication

Most people with asthma have to take **medication**. Some people take pills every day. Many others use an **inhaler** every day, or when they have an **attack**. An inhaler is a small container filled with medication. You breathe in the medication through a mouthpiece attached to the container.

Your doctor will tell you what kind of medication to take for your asthma. He or she will show you the right way to use an inhaler if you need one.

Your doctor will show you how to use an inhaler, and answer your questions about asthma. ▶

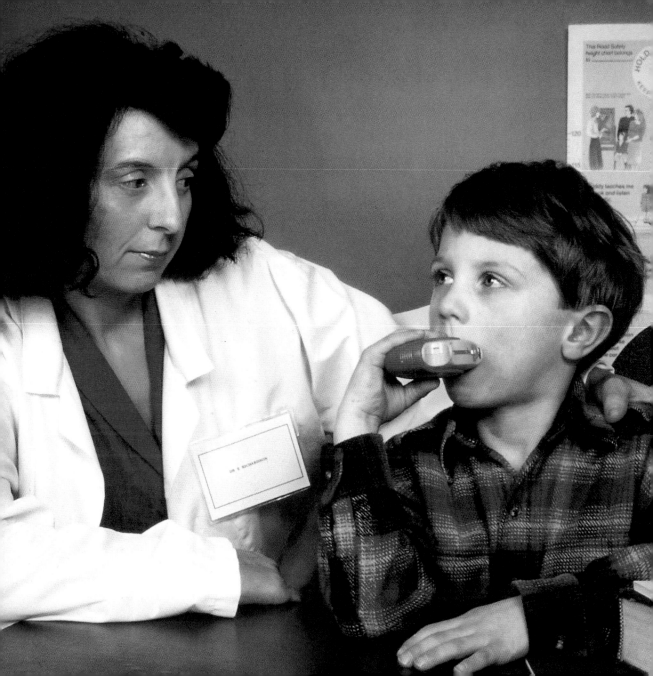

When medication is not enough

It's very important to take your **medication** when you're supposed to. But there may be times when it isn't enough to make you better. If this happens, you may have to go to hospital.

Although it may seem frightening, a stay in hospital will help you to feel well again. The doctors there will be able to stop your asthma **attack**.

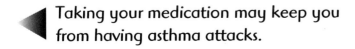
Taking your medication may keep you from having asthma attacks.

What can you do?

Do your best to keep asthma **attacks** from happening. Stay away from things that you're **allergic** to, like dogs, flowers or peanuts. If you find that heavy exercise brings on an attack, choose sports that don't include lots of running.

In time, you'll learn what to avoid and when you need your **medication**. Once you know how to control your asthma, you'll feel a lot better. And even if you do have an attack, you'll know how to help yourself.

It's a good idea to stay away from the things that you're allergic to.

At school

If you have **asthma**, you and your parents should tell your teachers. You can show them your **inhaler**, and explain when and how you need to use it. It's a good idea to give them your doctor's phone number, in case they ever need to get in touch with him or her.

Tell your teacher if certain exercises or sports make your asthma worse. They should also know if you're **allergic** to anything.

Using a **spacer**, a large container connected to your inhaler, can make it easier to breathe in your medication.

Glossary

allergic (a-LER-jik) – when something that's usually harmless gives you a bad **reaction**, such as sneezing or a rash. Some reactions can be very serious

allergy (AL-er-jee) – a bad **reaction** to something that's usually harmless

attack (a-TAK) – a time when asthma makes it hard to breathe

inhaler (in-HAY-ler) – a small container filled with **medication** that you breathe into your **lungs**

lungs – two spongy sacks in your chest that you breathe with. The sacks fill with air as you breathe in

medication (MED-i-kay-shun) – a chemical that helps your body

reaction (ree-AK-shun) – a response to something

spacer (SPAY-ser) – a large container that fits onto your **inhaler** to make it easier to breathe in the **medication**

Index